essentials

Springer essentials

Springer essentials provide up-to-date knowledge in a concentrated form. They aim to deliver the essence of what counts as "state-of-the-art" in the current academic discussion or in practice. With their quick, uncomplicated and comprehensible information, essentials provide:

- an introduction to a current issue within your field of expertis
- an introduction to a new topic of interest
- an insight, in order to be able to join in the discussion on a particular topic

Available in electronic and printed format, the books present expert knowledge from Springer specialist authors in a compact form. They are particularly suitable for use as eBooks on tablet PCs, eBook readers and smartphones. *Springer essentials* form modules of knowledge from the areas economics, social sciences and humanities, technology and natural sciences, as well as from medicine, psychology and health professions, written by renowned Springer-authors across many disciplines.

More information about this subseries at http://www.springer.com/series/16761

Reinhard Ematinger

From Industry 4.0 to Business Model 4.0

Opportunities of the Digital Transformation

 Springer

Reinhard Ematinger
Heidelberg, Germany

The translation was done with the help of artificial intelligence (machine translation by the service DeepL.com). A subsequent human revision was done primarily in terms of content.

ISSN 2197-6708   ISSN 2197-6716   (electronic)
essentials
ISSN 2731-3107   ISSN 2731-3115   (electronic)
Springer essentials
ISBN 978-3-658-32399-8   ISBN 978-3-658-32400-1   (eBook)
https://doi.org/10.1007/978-3-658-32400-1

This book is a translation of the original German edition „Von der Industrie 4.0 zum Geschäftsmodell 4.0" by Ematinger, Reinhard, published by Springer Fachmedien Wiesbaden GmbH in 2018.

This Springer imprint is published by the registered company Springer Fachmedien Wiesbaden GmbH part of Springer Nature.
The registered company address is: Abraham-Lincoln-Str. 46, 65189 Wiesbaden, Germany

What You Can Find in This *essential*

- Valuable impulses to benefit from the changed rules of the game and to discover patterns for new business models.
- Usable tools like the *Business Model Canvas* for creating, discussing, and testing business models.
- The Digital Matrix, with which you can "translate" developments in Industry 4.0 for utilizing them for your good ideas.

Contents

About the Authors

Text by Dr. Reinhard Ematinger Expert for Business Model Innovation, Heidelberg, hoi@ematinger.com, www.ematinger.com
Illustrations by Diplom-Designerin Sandra Schulze Graphic Recorder and Illustrator, Heidelberg, info@sandraschulze.com, www.sandraschulze.com

Introduction

1

The digitalization of the industry opens up new opportunities for companies of different sectors and sizes - and also brings new risks: There is the chance to develop new business models and to generate new revenues from the experience of the previous business with "old" and "new" customers. At the same time, there is the risk of losing the connection to existing customers because new competitors with more attractive business models and with significantly greater benefits for their customers are entering the game.

© Springer Fachmedien Wiesbaden GmbH, part of Springer Nature 2021
R. Ematinger, *From Industry 4.0 to Business Model 4.0*, Springer essentials,
https://doi.org/10.1007/978-3-658-32400-1_1

The Rules of the Game Have Changed 2

Digital business models are changing the market. Companies that fail to adapt to the rules of the game and technological possibilities will lose customers and sooner or later possibly their entire previous business.

Let's face it: In the upcoming years, we will see a noticeable change in many companies and many traditional business models (Fig. 2.1). Changing expectations of private and business customers and the question of the actual benefits for customers and suppliers - hand in hand with a sometimes dramatic technological change - mean that companies will have to deal with a number of issues:

- the future of so far unknown events,
- further disruptions with effects they cannot even guess,
- new competitors that they have not yet identified, and
- further products and services that are already transforming entire industries and will continue to do so.

© Springer Fachmedien Wiesbaden GmbH, part of Springer Nature 2021
R. Ematinger, *From Industry 4.0 to Business Model 4.0*, Springer essentials,
https://doi.org/10.1007/978-3-658-32400-1_2

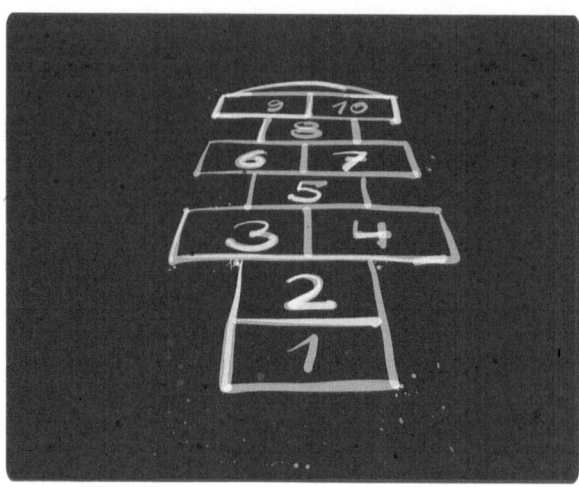

Fig. 2.1 Playing field and rules

A View into the Crystal Ball 4.0

This section offers five developments that not only make the elusive buzzword "Industry 4.0" a little more tangible, but also enables the fundamental change in digital integration in our day-to-day business. Customers and business partners expect that questions and answers about Industry 4.0 will be handled way less centrally in competence centers and that more roles, disciplines and functions will feel responsible for digitalization in organizations. A number of challenges still need to be overcome on the way of achieving this goal.

3.1 Fact about the Internet of Things

In its paper "A Guide to the Internet of Things: How Billions of Online Objects Are Making the Web Wiser," Intel counts a whopping 200 billion intelligent objects, from very small chips to very large machines, which will communicate wirelessly with each other and with us in 2020 (Intel 2015). That makes, to make the figure a little bit clearer, about 26 of these smart objects for every person on earth. The smart objects will provide the necessary data to determine stock levels in real time, control machines and systems, save costs and save lives. Intel refers to the McKinsey Global Institute and the New York Times and estimates the global added value of Internet of Things technology in 2025 at more than US$6 trillion—which is US$6000 billion.

© Springer Fachmedien Wiesbaden GmbH, part of Springer Nature 2021
R. Ematinger, *From Industry 4.0 to Business Model 4.0*, Springer essentials,
https://doi.org/10.1007/978-3-658-32400-1_3

3.2   Fact about Robots

The use of robots will increase by about 2000% between 2016 and 2030. The news portal Business Insider predicts a global market of around US$190 billion, which means that we talk of a huge market with the potential to make life easier for us consumers (Business Insider 2014). There will be at least three serious hurdles along the way:

- Firstly, we tend to find robots that are too human-like strange at best,
- Secondly, the available technology will continue to be very expensive; and
- Thirdly, issues related to privacy and the protection of intellectual property are not resolved.

Whether and when we will overcome these hurdles will be shown by progress achieved in the coming years. Exciting initiatives such as the 3D print of a steel pedestrian bridge in Amsterdam depicted in Fig. 3.1 illustrate how robotic support can be used in the future to design in an efficient, economic and safe way (von Schoenebeck 2015).

3.3   Fact about Interfaces

In the TechCrunch article "The Battle Is for the Customer Interface," Tom Goodwin emphasizes the importance of the interface between the supply and the demand side (Goodwin 2015). Companies like Twitter and Facebook represent wafer-thin

Fig. 3.1 Robots print steel bridge

interfaces between suppliers and their processes on the one hand (where the costs are located) and a vast number of customers on the other (where the revenues are located). Companies like Tesla or Nest, on the other hand, strive to have constant control over all "layers": research, development, production, marketing and sales. This offers quite a lot of options to keep the revenues within the company, but is much more difficult to scale in a sustainable way. Newspaper publishers have to write, check facts, buy equipment and paper, and print and deliver their products. Platforms such as Facebook, on the other hand, "only" offer platforms for their users who create their own content, and Twitter makes money by linking to the frontpage of the newspapers.

3.4   Fact about Generations

While many employers still often react helplessly to Generation Y and its actual and traditional demands, companies are preparing for Generation Z, whose members are slowly entering the labor market (Solis 2015). This generation, born between 1995 and 2010, which detractors attest the attention span of a goldfish - Jeremy Finch of design firm Altitude calls it an "8-second filter" in his report - has already developed the ability to filter and sort enormous amounts of information (Finch 2015). It seeks acceptance in social media, but has a fine instinct of whether and when attention is worthwhile, and is then thoroughly focused and binding (Zipkin 2015). This generation will find itself between two chairs: on the one hand, they need social media to find confirmation and build their personal brand, and on the other hand, they want to differentiate themselves and not be defined solely by their perception in the internet (see Fig. 3.2). Brands and companies that understand this area of conflict will become attractive as employers and suppliers.

3.5   Fact about Financing

Crowdfunding will increase by 200,000% by 2030 as an alternative or supplement to the classic form of fundraising, says JT Ripton from the SAP Center for Business Insight (Ripton 2015). Especially for small companies with big ideas, the seemingly endless approval processes of established banks and venture capitalists are not the very best alternative for obtaining financing. Platforms such as Kickstarter and Indiegogo make it possible to raise money from many investors and to control the entire process yourself - with the desired side effect of creating enormous reach

Fig. 3.2 Generation Z

in the communication of your own idea and offer. The "story" behind the offer to be financed is a central element: crowdfunding platforms are made for good storytelling. Good sellers are able to sell almost any existing product or service. However, selling thousands of units of an offer that does not yet exist in reality is only possible for those who attract our attention and interest, who inspire us and invite us to be part of an exciting journey.

Why We Need a New Understanding of Processes

Industry 4.0 will enable not less than a revolution in business processes and business models, and the interaction between people and IT will be redefined in already clearly emerging Industry 4.0 scenarios, corresponding to new internal and external processes. More responsibility will lie in conducting and orchestrating processes that happen in real time and hand in hand with intelligent machines and systems. Entire process landscapes are currently changing due to digitalization and networking, and they will continue to do so in the future. So much for theory. And the practice: In order to be successful with new concepts and tools and to raise potentials, detailed knowledge of one's own current and possible future internal processes and those of customers and suppliers is necessary (IBM 2015).

The author chooses five promising patterns outlined in Fig. 4.1, defines them, gives advantages and examples of use and asks you to note your thoughts on how to "translate" these patterns into your current and future offerings. The "What does it mean for you?" boxes in the following sections make the explanations relevant to your offerings and provide you with appropriate questions to help the transfer into the reality of your organization.

4.1 Real-Time Processes

They make optimization of interactions with business partners possible by running huge volumes of transactions simultaneously and ensuring a real-time overview of the entire logistics chain, for example. Data such as stock levels, transport times or

© Springer Fachmedien Wiesbaden GmbH, part of Springer Nature 2021
R. Ematinger, *From Industry 4.0 to Business Model 4.0*, Springer essentials,
https://doi.org/10.1007/978-3-658-32400-1_4

Fig. 4.1 Five patterns for business processes

production statuses are always available just as up-to-date as analyses of the profit-ability of individual products and services. The advantages of shorter cycles for business processes lie in better use of assets, faster closing of fiscal years or higher customer loyalty. By using intelligent sensors, motorcycle manufacturer Harley-Davidson has succeeded in continuously analyzing production data and determin-ing the time required for individual production steps to the nearest tenth of a sec-ond (Christ 2014). The machines in the production line communicate with each other and are capable of producing 1700 product variants on one line. This enables Harley-Davidson to manufacture significantly more products and to reduce the delivery times of individual motorcycles from the previous 21 days to now 6 hours (Mulholland 2015).

What Does this Mean for you?

- Which of your processes can you accelerate noticeably?
- Which of these will your customers notice (and reward)?
- Could you reach additional customer segments?

4.2   Forward-Looking Processes

They support companies in making more intelligent decisions by, for example, in-tegrating them with ERP systems to record the status of production plants with sensors, detect possible failures in advance and initiate corrective measures in real time. External data from business partners, statistics portals, weather stations, event calendars, agencies, or social media also help companies to perform accurate demand forecasts, optimize inventories, send out customized offers at the right time, and reduce out-of-stock rates. The advantages lie in more efficient use of re-sources, higher productivity and lower costs. Sportswear manufacturer Under

Armour can predict customer behavior by correlating shoppers' individual transactions with seasonal, weekly and daily patterns (Smiley 2016; Cao and Cortez 2016).

What Does this Mean for You?

- Which processes could you transform into predictive processes?
- What will your current and future customers gain from this?
- How do you estimate both the initial and ongoing costs and the benefits?

4.3 Lean Processes

They optimize business processes by reducing process steps or by automation, on the one hand to meet customer requirements for individual, high-quality products and services and fast response to orders, on the other to avoid bottlenecks or delays in supply. Among other things, the aim is to continuously reduce direct and indirect costs by identifying relevant cost drivers and waste in existing processes. The advantages of coordinating the processes in procurement, production and sales are increased profitability and delivery capability and the long-term safeguarding of the knowledge available in the company. The Chilean mining company Codelco founded a digital subsidiary in 2003, developed a vision for the future of its operations and automated its four copper mines as part of the "Codelco 2.0" initiative. Driverless transporters, remote-controlled mining of the rock and real-time information of all relevant data are the results of the initiative (Westermann et al. 2016).

What Does this Mean for You?

- Which internal processes can you streamline without too much effort?
- What do you get out of it? What do your customers get out of it?
- Which cost blocks could you reduce by when?

4.4 Enriched Processes

They use contextual data from a variety of sources to streamline operations and offer users countless ways to interact with companies and products. Suppliers use interactive content such as videos or games to gain insights into customer prefer-

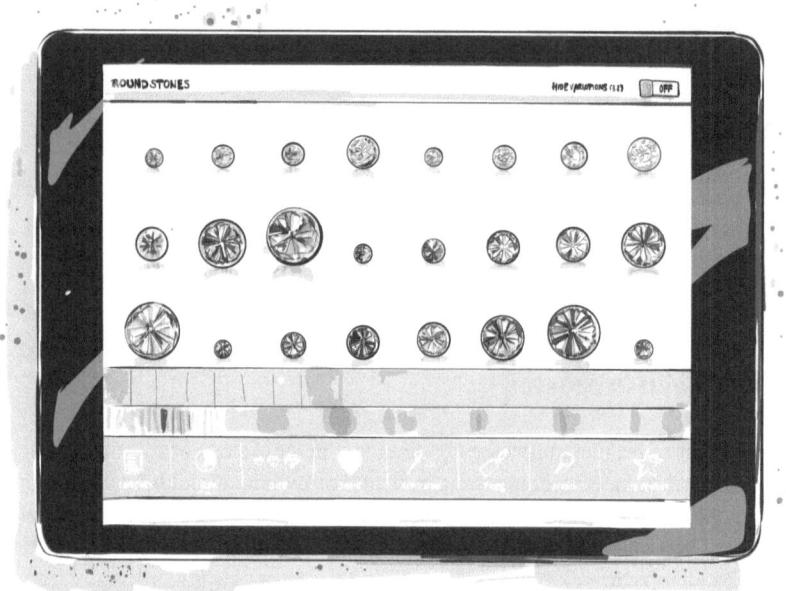

Fig. 4.2 Swarovski's "Crystal Collection" app. (European Design 2017)

ences and are able to translate these insights into customized communication and ideas for future products. The advantages lie on one hand in the higher probability of turning prospects with relevant offers into customers and on the other hand in the reduction of customer churn. The Austrian company Swarovski offers B2B customers more than 15,000 variations of its crystals and over 400,000 other elements (Swarovski 2017). This variety could hardly be presented with standard presentation material: Before the "Crystal Collection" app for smartphones and tablets was presented, only about 10% of the available collection could be experienced by customers. The app shown in Fig. 4.2 makes it possible to interactively show every available product variant, display availability and delivery times and offer new products without delay. Insights into the preferences of B2B customers can be used to develop new products.

What Does this Mean for you?

- Which activities can you reduce through enriched processes?
- Can you save time, for example in product design? How?
- Can you turn more prospects into loyal customers this way?

4.5 Self-Learning Processes

They use the "thinking" and "learning" of machines that draw on a pool of experience from collected data in order to make independent decisions and adapt processes. Patterns in customer behavior can also be recognized in order to generate customized offers more quickly and increase the probability of a purchase. The advantages are the reduction of throughput times in production and an increase in revenues. The Fraunhofer Institute for Process Engineering and Packaging (Fraunhofer-Institut für Verfahrenstechnik und Verpackung) is developing a self-learning automation system for efficient cleaning: In order to maintain high hygienic standards in food production, production facilities must be continuously checked and cleaned without dismantling them. Although the cleaning process is thorough, it is oversized, consuming too much water, detergents and time. In the future, machines will recognize how polluted they are and independently decide how much water, detergents and time to use for cleaning (Bargs-Stahl 2016). With this process, production facilities will be cleaned in a hygienically perfect and environmentally friendly manner and downtimes will be reduced.

What Does this Mean for you?

- Which process steps could you save in this way? Why and how?
- Could you react quickly to changing markets this way?
- Do your customers accept pricing based on demand?

Why We Need a New Understanding of Business Models

Sustainable business models and inspiring customer benefits are the key to long-term success for a company: Realizing entrepreneurial opportunities in a more uncertain and complex business world is a crucial competitive advantage. Innovation that is limited to technology alone does not guarantee success. New products and services should be meaningfully coupled with business models that define the market entry strategies as well as the benefits for key customer segments.

In his contribution on the limits and opportunities of business model innovations, Henry Chesbrough points out that the economic benefits of a technology remain limited as long as they are not commercialized by a working business model (Chesbrough 2010). The authors of the IBM CEO study also emphasize that over the past 10 years, executives have had to observe how digitalization and other trends have made some business models obsolete. "For CEOs, this means that they must fundamentally change their portfolio, business model, way of working and long-held beliefs. They need to pay more attention to what is important to customers today and reassess the way they create value," the authors write in their wake-up call (IBM 2010). The results of the study, conducted across 32 industries, show that almost all CEOs are adapting the business models of their organizations: 69% of respondents confirmed that they will make significant efforts toward business model innovation in the next 3 years.

To address current and future threats and create new revenue models, companies not only have to understand their business models (which are much harder to copy than products and services because they consist of customer value, critical resources, and a unique ecosystem of customers, customers' customers, partners,

© Springer Fachmedien Wiesbaden GmbH, part of Springer Nature 2021   15
R. Ematinger, *From Industry 4.0 to Business Model 4.0*, Springer essentials,
https://doi.org/10.1007/978-3-658-32400-1_5

Fig. 5.1 Five patterns for business models

and suppliers, among other things), but also adapt, communicate, and implement them in real-life.

In analogy to the business processes in the previous section, the author also selects five patterns of business models shown in Fig. 5.1, defines them and presents examples of applications and enterprises. Feel free to write down your thoughts on how to "translate" the patterns into your current and future offers.

5.1   Selling Results Instead of Products

Companies charge for the use of their products or the results achieved with them—such as reduction of the total cost of ownership or the operating hours worked. Clear agreements between suppliers and customers as well as clear definitions of achievable results and their measurement are necessary for this.

John Deere, who manufactures agricultural, construction, as well as forestry machinery, diesel engines, and drivetrains, offers the option of paying for the operating hours of its combine harvesters, which saves the farmer high investments and maintenance of the machines (John Deere 2017). Rolls-Royce, too, has been charging customers such as Boeing and Airbus since 1962 for the operating hours flown as an alternative to individual engines with its "power-by-the-hour" offer (Rolls-Royce 2012). The aircraft turbines remain the property of Rolls-Royce, which also handles their maintenance and repair. Recurring revenues are generated by charging for flying hours. Thus, the previously divergent interests of the business units responsible for development, production and service are now united in one goal—to offer engines that require as little maintenance as possible.

What Does this Mean for you?

- Which of your offers could you charge according to usage?
- What exactly would you have to do? What would be the cost?
- Could you win new promising customers?

5.2   Overcoming Previous Industry Boundaries

Companies are expanding their offers into other, sometimes completely foreign, industry sectors. This pattern is often based on the key resources and activities of a manufacturer.

The example of Tesla with its Powerwall—a rechargeable battery for private households that is designed to compensate for fluctuations in the grid caused by the use of solar and wind power—clearly shows this (Martin 2016). The Tesla model is also based on alliances and acquisitions: In the summer of 2016, Tesla took over the "green" power manufacturer Solarcity in order to jointly manufacture solar plants and battery storage systems in addition to electric cars (Tesla Team 2016). The plan is to offer electrically powered buses and trucks as well as mobility services in its own years.

Other companies that have more or less recently entered the market, such as Airbnb and Uber, question the status quo of the respective industry with its established players: German paper "brand eins" author Thomas Ramge notes in an article that "Disruption means interruption, meaning the destruction of traditional business models and value chains." He cites Steve Jobs and Apple's iTunes Store as role models, as they prove how disruptive innovation and expansion across previous industry boundaries works (Ramge 2015).

What Does this Mean for you?

• Which industry boundaries and definitions are obsolete? Why?
• In which foreign industry would you like to expand? Who stands in your way?
• Which partners do you need to take your first steps? When?

5.3   Acting on the Market as a Network

Companies use the knowledge, resources and established ecosystems of their partners to increase the benefits for their customers in a given network. Plus, if they share common quality standards and transparent revenue models, they can simultaneously focus on their respective expertise and expand their competencies.

An exciting example is the Innocentive platform, founded in 2001, with which innovation can be "outsourced" (Innocentive 2017). The focus of the platform is on complex scientific questions, and the tasks advertised to the more than 375,000 researchers, technicians and designers are correspondingly demanding. The German suitcase manufacturer Rimowa wants to save business travelers and frequent flyers long waiting times when checking in their luggage, and from sticking paper tags onto their suitcases. Together with Lufthansa, Airbus, T-Systems and Netronix, the company developed the "Electronic Tag" which allows passengers to check in their luggage via app from home or on the road: In addition to the boarding pass, passengers also receive the baggage data via app, which the app sends from their smartphone to their suitcase via Bluetooth. A display on the suitcase immediately shows the transmitted information and the checked-in baggage can be placed on the conveyor belt at the airport and automatically transported to the aircraft (see Fig. 5.2). The cooperation with Lufthansa has already started, cooperations with United, Condor, Eva Air and Thomas Cook are in the test phase (Lufthansa 2016).

• What added value could you create—together with your partners—for "old" and "new" customers?
• Whom do you need for this? Which first steps would be necessary?
• What kind of new internal resources do you need for this? Why?

Fig. 5.2 Digital luggage tag from Rimowa

5.4   Availability Instead of Ownership

Companies like Uber, Airbnb, Meine Ernte and TaskRabbit act as platforms for supply and demand without actually owning vehicles, real estate, vegetable plots or manpower. Sharing, exchanging or renting instead of buying is both an old cultural technique and a new trend.

JustPark, a company financed by BMW i Ventures, among others, uses the "Sharing Economy Index" to research a list of offers: almost 900 entries are currently listed in categories such as "borrow," "buy," "exchange" and "share" (Just Park 2017). A study by the consulting firm PwC comes to the conclusion that more than 80% of Germans under 30 have already taken advantage of a sharing offer and that sharing and borrowing as an alternative to buying will become more widespread—across all age groups: more than 60% of those surveyed stated that they would like to use Sharing Economy offers in the future (PwC 2015). DriveNow, a company founded in 2011 by BMW and Sixt, leases its fleet to more than 500,000 customers in Europe, thus offering an alternative to owning a car in large cities and, as a desirable side effect, reducing the fear of e-mobility.

What Does this Mean for you?

• Do customers turn away because they no longer want to own your products?
• Can you change your revenue models? Which ones and at which cost?
• Which key resources are no longer needed? Why?

5.5   Digitalization of Products and Services

Companies are either digitalizing previously "analog" products such as books and music and realize savings in production, warehousing and logistics, or are using technologies such as 3D printing to produce physical products according to short-term demand.

The Handelsblatt publishing group offers a great case study of a working pattern: in 2013, the publishing group launched its live app, which supplemented the highest-circulation German-language business and financial newspaper with individual digital articles. By expanding paid content and further developing its digital offers, the publishing group was able to increase the use of its online products and tap into new revenue streams. With the "Handelsblatt Digital Pass" introduced in

2014, more than 30,000 customers are granted access to all paid-content articles, e-paper, Handelsblatt Live, dossiers, and the archive, in addition to membership in the Business Club and preferential conditions at events. With the "Handelsblatt 10" payment app launched in 2016, the flood of news is reduced to the ten most important topics, delivered daily at 16.30 (TBO 2017). The ten news items are synchronized and offer a comprehensive overview of the news situation in a nutshell—and thus correspond to the rather limited reading time of stressed railway passengers.

What Does this Mean for you?

- Can you digitalize parts of your portfolio? With which ones could you start?
- Which customer segments could you "move" to digital products?
- Can you offer added value to existing customers and attract new ones?

How to Create a Viable Basis for Future Business Models

6

Understanding your own business model is both a challenge and one of the most important assets of an organization, whether it is a start-up or an established company. However, when executives are asked to explain their current business model, most answers are vague at best and have more to do with corporate structure and processes than with the "logic" of the business. This "logic" has changed again and again since industrialization, has been adapted, discarded and developed anew, but with current technical and organizational possibilities, the speed and pressure on the people and organizations involved are increasing.

Business models are not fixed stars, but have to be continuously adapted to reality: Competitors are added, products that supplement or replace the own portfolio are appearing, ingredients of the own service offerings become obsolete and possible partners offer new access to prospects and customers and thus create new revenue models.

The author is convinced that it is therefore worthwhile to regularly review, optimize and redesign the essential building blocks of your own business model and those of your most important customers and partners.

6.1   The Business Model Canvas

The Business Model Canvas, developed by Alexander Osterwalder and Yves Pigneur and described in the bestselling book "Business Model Generation," has developed since 2009 into a standard format that can be used in many industries to

© Springer Fachmedien Wiesbaden GmbH, part of Springer Nature 2021   21
R. Ematinger, *From Industry 4.0 to Business Model 4.0*, Springer essentials,
https://doi.org/10.1007/978-3-658-32400-1_6

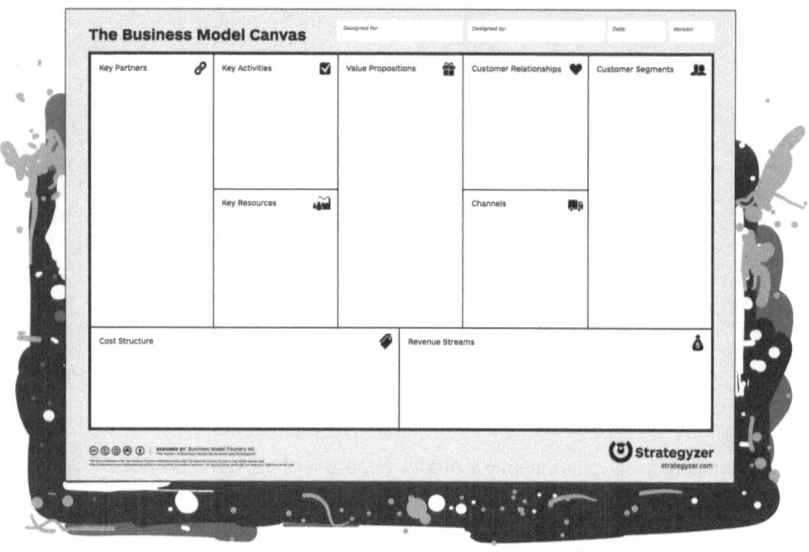

Fig. 6.1   Business Model Canvas

describe business models in a comprehensible way (Osterwalder and Pigneur 2010). The Business Model Canvas shown in Fig. 6.1 on one hand provides clarity for an as-is analysis of the current business model and, on the other hand, forms a tangible starting point for the development, discussion, validation and selection of possible future business models. It is based on nine building blocks that represent the four important areas of an organization—whether it is a start-up, a nonprofit or a corporation:

- the most important customers,
- the tangible value propositions of the own offering,
- the necessary infrastructure, and
- financial viability.

The Business Model Canvas is processed in the order shown below with the nine building blocks shown in Fig. 6.1. Building Blocks 1 to 5 represent the "front-stage" area facing the customer and perceived by him, and building blocks 6 to 9 represent the "backstage" area located in the background:

- Building block 1—the customer segments: The roles of different persons or groups in organizations for which a company wants to create value propositions are outlined here. It makes sense to divide customers into different segments if their needs and demands require individual offerings, if they are reached via different sales channels, if they require different types of relationships, if their purchasing behavior and price sensitivity are different, if their willingness to invest or their knowledge is different and if they are differently profitable for the supplier.
- Building block 2—the value propositions: This block describes how specific problems are solved or needs of the respective customer segments are satisfied by creating a tangible benefit with products or services. A value proposition in itself never describes the functionality of products or services or the components of a requirements specification, but always the actual value for the customer.
- Building block 3—the channels: This block describes the communication-, distribution- and sales channels through which a company communicates and delivers its value to its previously defined customer segments. Here, too, the focus is on the value delivered to the customers and not so much on the product or service.
- Building block 4 – the customer relationships: This block answers the question of how the relationships that a company maintains or intends to maintain with its most important customer segments are structured. Different variants are conceivable, ranging from individual support, communities and chat support to no special support.
- Building block 5—the revenue streams: This block answers the question of what benefits the individual customer segments are prepared to pay for. Here, the type of revenue is essential, not individual amounts or figures, for example, the billing of a service per hour or day, the sale of a product per thousand units, a flat rate or even a free service.
- Building block 6—the key resources: The most important tangible and intangible resources that are necessary for the functioning of the outlined business model are described here. These may include machinery and equipment, buildings, raw materials as well as unique knowledge of the employees, registered patents, trademarks or a loyal customer base.
- Building block 7—the key activities: This block contains the key activities that an organization undertakes to create the value proposition described above for the most important customer segments. In a start-up phase, these will be other activities—such as social marketing, finding investors and maintaining press contacts—than in established companies.

- Building block 8—the key partners: This block describes the network of partners who contribute to the success of the business model. People and organizations outside your own organization—such as joint venture companies, suppliers, the press, bloggers, even competitors who are needed to make the business model successful—can be potential current or future partners.
- Building block 9—the cost structure: The last building block describes the costs resulting from activities, resources and partnerships in the implementation of the business model. For a common understanding of the business model, it is also useful to distinguish between variable and fixed costs. Analogous to the revenue streams, the type of costs is important, as opposed to individual amounts or figures.

The presented building blocks of the Business Model Canvas offer companies out of different industry sectors in different phases an out-of-the-box usable transparent foundation to ensure a common understanding of the current business model and to create a starting point for future scenarios.

The author asks you to write down your thoughts on the nine building blocks of the Business Model Canvas in order to "translate" this logic into your organization's current and future offers, and provides you five questions each.

What Does this Mean for you?
Five questions on building block 1 (customer segments)

- Which customer segments are particularly important for you? Why?
- Who benefits from your range of products or services particularly?
- Do you actually reach the "right" contact persons? Are you sure?
- What untapped niches are out there that could be attractive for you?
- How could you segment your key target markets differently?

Five questions on building block 2 (value propositions)

- What concrete benefit do your offerings have for the most important customers?
- What problems do you solve with your products or services?
- What added value could complementary offers provide?
- What can you change in your offerings to better emphasize the USP?
- How could you adapt your offerings to the most important customer segments?

Five questions on building block 3 (channels)

- How do your products or services get to your most important customers?
- How do your customers learn about your offerings? Where and when?
- Do you address the advantages of your offerings in a comprehensible way?
- How could you use social media sensibly without a lot of effort?
- How do you make it easy for key customers to buy your offerings?

Five questions on building block 4 (customer relationships)

- How do you organize the relationships with your customers as efficiently as possible?
- What kind of relationship do your key customer segments expect?
- Do you collect references from enthusiastic customers? How do you do that?
- What part of your customer relationships can be automated?
- How could we give our customers an active role with us?

Five questions on building block 5 (revenue streams)

- What exactly do your customers pay for? Are you sure?
- What are the realistic options for cross- and upselling?
- Could you offer your customers more attractive conditions?
- What other revenue streams and types of revenue can you think of?
- Can and do you want to make prices dependent on demand?

Five questions on building block 6 (key resources)

- Do you also think of intangible resources such as trademarks and patents?
- How do you ensure that these resources are up to date?
- How big is your risk that your most important resources will be copied?
- Which important qualifications are needed in order not to stand still?
- Could you benefit from your key resources in a new way?

Five questions on building block 7 (key activities)

- Which of your activities generate the greatest added value for your customers?
- Which of your previous activities is an obstacle to further growth?
- Which of your activities impair the efficiency desired or required?
- What should you continue to do yourself, to outsource or to purchase? Why?
- In which activities could you involve your most important customers?

Five questions on building block 8 (key partners)

- Who are your most important partners? Why? What are they doing for you?
- What benefits and value do you offer your most important partners?
- Do your partners understand the "logic" of your business model? Do they?
- How could old and new partners help to reach new customers?
- On which of your partners are you dependent (too) strongly? Why?

Five questions on building block 9 (cost structure):

- What are the largest cost blocks in your business model?
- How could you cut costs without reducing the level of your services?
- Can you convert fixed costs into variable costs? How and when?
- Which financial risks can you reduce? How?
- Can you achieve economies of scale? How do you approach this?

6.2   Connection to Industry 4.0

In order to meet the context of Industry 4.0 and to transfer the most important topics of business model innovation to these scenarios, the author proposes to include the following specifics in the considerations:

- Looking at an organization's environment: In Industry 4.0 scenarios, value creation should not be understood as a one-way process toward supplier—own company—customer—customer of the customer in the customer segments defined above. Among other things, value is created simultaneously in several directions for customers, for customers of customers, and for partners, so it is necessary to broaden the view from one's own organization to the entire ecosystem.
- Extending the customer benefit to all partners involved: In line with the above point, when outlining new business models you may want to ensure that the interests of all partners involved are taken into account. Since in Industry 4.0 scenarios all stakeholders usually have expressed or unspoken motivation to build and maintain a network, the benefits for all parties involved should be explicitly outlined when developing feasible business models.
- Capturing synergies for the entire network: A mere linear view of creating and maintaining value for customers and partners does not make too much sense in

Industry 4.0 scenarios. This point also builds upon the previous ones—it is necessary to outline and discuss the assumptions about interrelationships, dependencies and synergies as a network rather than as a line.

- Include data as additional key resources: Since most Industry 4.0 scenarios involve the collection and processing of huge amounts of data, it is appropriate to consider this data as additional key resources. On the one hand, the collected data can create additional customer value within existing business models and be translated into additional revenue streams for suppliers, and on the other hand, completely new business models can be created by using this data.

- Including intelligent objects as additional key resources: In both business-to-consumer and business-to-business scenarios, countless digitally networked intelligent objects—from sensors and RFID chips to drones, 3D printers and robots and autonomous vehicles – will obviously enter the playground. They automatically interact with each other and with people, and they create, process and connect digital and even physical objects. In this way, they create additional benefits for the network and its players described above and should therefore be considered as another important resource when discussing future business models.

How to Combine Building Blocks of your Business Model and Digital Elements into the Digital Matrix

In order to complete the specifics of business ideas and models discussed above in the context of Industry 4.0 into a usable and understandable structure, to discuss to—be— and as—is—situations and to derive possible next steps of implementation, it would be useful to combine the most important building blocks of a business model with the key elements of digitalization.

The following three elements form the vertical axis of the Digital Matrix as shown in Fig. 7.1:

- Element 1—networked people: People in the digital economy are well informed and use digital applications in different ways as a matter of course. Stationary and mobile computers, smartphones or smart watches connect them with other people via online communities and social networks. As customers, they leave digital traces in the form of data and thus form the foundation of many digital business processes and models. In Industry 4.0, they provide impulses to promote innovation in their organizations in responsible roles: they transform existing business through the use of digital technologies and help open up new revenue sources. They bring in impulses from foreign industries, focus on customer benefits beyond products and services and put current business models to the test.
- Element 2—intelligent objects: While objects were rather stupid in the past, they are now increasingly part of the digital world and, as described in the section "Fact about Internet of Things," they interact intelligently with people, whole organizations or other objects. Intelligent objects are usually equipped with sensors, produce data and sometimes have their own application logic.

R. Ematinger, *From Industry 4.0 to Business Model 4.0*, Springer essentials,
https://doi.org/10.1007/978-3-658-32400-1_7

Fig. 7.1 Three digital elements

Fig. 7.2 Five building blocks of the business model

They are able to react automatically to events or other intelligent objects (such as customers' smartphones) in the respective B2C context. In Industry 4.0, we include robots, drones, autonomous vehicles and components of digital production such as 3D printers, which create benefits by automatically exchanging information. In the chapter "Why we need a new understanding of processes," the author already described possible uses of intelligent objects and their benefits.

- Element 3—services and data in the cloud: We understand the public, corporate or private cloud and its services and processed data for our further consideration less as technological infrastructure but as a value—added service. Value that contributes to the business model is created as people and intelligent objects digitally connect in real time, collect and exchange data and, in conjunction with physical objects or exclusively digitally, generate information. For our consideration, we use Big Data and Smart Data synonymously. Big Data is "large amounts of data from a variety of sources with a high processing speed," Smart Data gives "users the opportunity (...) to select from a potentially very large and heterogeneous mass of data exactly the data that is relevant for the current context" (Bitkom 2015; Memmel 2015).

The five "frontstage" building blocks of Osterwalder's Business Model Canvas described in Sect. 6.1 form the horizontal axis of the Digital Matrix, as shown in Fig. 7.2:

- Building block 1—customer segments: The roles of the most important people for the digital business model are defined here. A maximum of five customer segments is quite sufficient for a first consideration. The maintenance manager and the production controller of a chemical company are customer segments that are of interest for the offering of a measurement technology manufacturer in that they are both interested in the digitalization of measurement results and the cross—company exchange of data.
- Building block 2—value propositions: The essential benefits for the previously defined customer segments are outlined in the context of the digital business model. Although entries may overlap, at least one value proposition is required per customer segment. The value proposition to plant operators of being able to monitor process parameters is pure functionality, as is the option of being able to detect wear and tear due to corrosion or deposition in real time. A tangible benefit arises for the respective customer segments results only with the associated increase in production efficiency, namely concrete cost savings or higher plant availability.
- Building block 3—channels: The analog and digital communication, distribution— and sales channels of a company are described here. Here, too, at least one relevant channel is required per customer segment. Companies that invest in their own highly qualified sales teams—that are committed to maintaining and intensifying contact with customers understand the metrics by which their customers measure results and success—are more likely to be perceived as trusted partners than vendors that offer only anonymous support and work with external sales agents.
- Building block 4—customer relationships: This building block describes the relationships that a company establishes with the previously defined customer segments. At least one type of relationship should be named for each customer segment. Account managers who provide long—term support to large industrial customers and are interested in partnership—based cooperation, joint enhancement of the product range or development of an industry standard, can make a significant contribution to the joint development of new digital business models.
- Building block 5—revenue streams: This building block describes the type of revenue for the respective customer segments. It is not necessary and sometimes not possible to define a revenue stream for each customer segment. Just paying for the usage of tools can be a more interesting model for customers in the construction industry than owning a machine park, as initial costs and expenses for repairs are eliminated and monthly fixed costs are easier to calculate: This is just one example of the "translation" of business model patterns across industries.

7.1   The Digital Matrix

The Digital Matrix shown in Fig. 7.3 now puts the five building blocks of the business model into a meaningful relationship with the three key elements of digitalization: networked people, intelligent objects, and services and data in the cloud as a vertical axis are now connected with customer segments, value propositions, channels, customer relationships, and revenue streams as a horizontal axis.

The author names and describes the essential "generators" that create added value in the context of digital business processes and models, gives examples and again asks you to note your thoughts on each of the three questions for a smooth "translation" into your organization's current and future offerings. In a book of this scope, these questions can only be generic and independent of the industry and its rules of the game, the region and the customers you serve. Therefore, the author asks for your understanding if one or the other question seems to be of little relevance to your current offering at first glance. It may be worthwhile to take a closer look at these very questions and give them a chance to be useful for the development of your future offering.

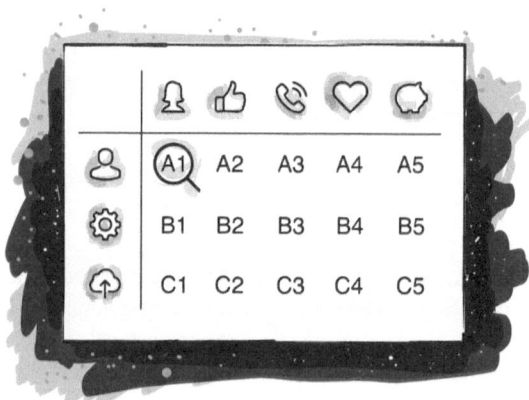

Fig. 7.3 Digital Matrix, example of the field "A1: Customer segments—networked people"

7.2   Customer Segments and Networked People (Field A1)

Existing and new customers become more and more mobile and "digital" thanks to smartphones, communities on the network can be considered either as one or more than one customer segments. Customers can obtain more favorable conditions by bundling their purchases. Apps such as Parkmobile make it possible to use smartphones in several cities to pay parking fees, and the B2B marketplace Ariba allows companies to easily collaborate with different partners in different regions.

What Does this Mean for you?

- Which new customer segments can you address with mobile devices and applications?
- What additional information can you gain by using digital technologies?
- Does it make sense to enable price—sensitive customers to bundle their purchases? What does this do to your brand?

7.3   Customer Segments and Intelligent Objects (Field B1)

Intelligent objects can autonomously take advantage of services and thus become "customers", too. In 2015, Budweiser introduced the Bud—E Fridge in the USA, a networked refrigerator that provides beer replenishment at the push of a button and lets you know when the stored beer has reached the optimum drinking temperature.

What Does this Mean for you?

- Can and should intelligent objects "order" services autonomously?
- How do you "reach" intelligent objects with tailor—made subscription offers?
- Can these intelligent objects recommend services to other intelligent objects or people?

7.4   Customer Segments and Services and Data in the Cloud (Field C1)

Regional offerings of companies can be provided directly and globally to the customer thanks to the digitalization of products and services. The online retailer geileweine.de aims to offer the best shopping experience with the best (regional) wines from the first contact in the shop to the enjoyment of the product and offers its products according to what they call "wine moments" and occasions for the perfect wine.

What Does this Mean for you?

• Which new customer segments can you reach with what effort and by when?
• How could you expand your existing customer base with useful cloud services?
• Do you need to adapt your offer, for example, depending on region, legal framework or customer segment?

7.5   Value Propositions and Networked People (Field A2)

Customers learn from the experiences of other customers because they can quickly gain a comprehensive overview of their opinions on products and services. This generates added value for online merchants such as Amazon, too, as these reviews help more interested parties to gain confidence in their decision and become buyers. The digital connections of people and companies established via LinkedIn often create added value for both sides and can result in new networks, products or services. The German online service ProvenExpert.com finds that recommendations from satisfied customers are the best way to successfully market services and offers customizable templates for customer reviews in different industries.

What Does this Mean for you?

• How can you create direct connections to prospects and customers to receive direct feedback on your offer?
• How could you create added value by connecting your customers to each other?
• Which new product and service offerings that are attractive to your customers can you create by connecting different providers—possibly even competitors?

7.6   Value Propositions and Intelligent Objects (Field B2)

Intelligent objects make it easier to collect and process the data necessary for an optimal solution in the customer's interest. Deutsche Telekom's Magenta SmartHome solution not only benefits customers, but also the partner network through the multi—vendor platform Qivicon.

What Does this Mean for you?

• Which intelligent objects are currently—and possibly in the future—relevant for the respective industries of your customers and for you?
• How could you design the interaction with intelligent objects in such a way that it is perceived as pleasant by your customers?
• How can you integrate intelligent properties into your existing product or service portfolio?

7.7   Value Propositions and Services and Data in the Cloud (Field C2)

Digitalization "dematerializes" previously physical products and ensures that supply can be adapted to current demand. Cloud—based networks create additional benefits for their customers by sharing data and combining services—including those of cooperating providers. Providers such as Netflix, which was founded as an online video store and film distributor and producer, deliver "on demand" by making content available to their subscribers via streaming. Providers such as Apple Pay or Paydirekt, a joint project of German banks, integrate the payment process in shops and online shops in such a way that the process is secure, fast and simple from the customer's perspective.

What Does this Mean for you?

• What actual benefits does a digital product offer to you and to your key customers and what is the added value compared to a physical product?
• Does your offer scale effortlessly or is substantial investment in additional resources necessary?

- What activities do you need to undertake to create individualized offers for your most important customer segments?

7.8   Channels and Networked People (Field A3)

Existing communication— and sales channels that connect suppliers and customers are supplemented and extended by intuitively designed digital interfaces and user interfaces. Companies can tailor their communication with the communities more precisely and unerringly. Platforms such as LinkedIn and XING offer partners and recruiters the information contained in their users' profiles, similar to the way B2B online marketplaces link supply and demand.

What Does this Mean for you?

- How can you use mobile devices to provide attractive access to your offerings for your key customers?
- How do you supplement or create new channels to your most important customer segments with current developments such as augmented reality?
- How do the profile data of the users of professional platforms contribute to a targeted communication between your customers and you?

7.9   Channels and Intelligent Objects (Field B3)

Intelligent objects offer additional access for suppliers to offer, sell and deliver products and services to their customers. As intelligent objects become more and more independent of users, they save their time, make maintenance plannable and ensure maximum availability of products and services. The German company symmedia offers an intelligent spare parts shop that networks production facilities with the manufacturer of the machines. Based on machine data, a shopping cart with order suggestions is automatically created and original spare parts can be ordered with just one click.

What Does this Mean for you?

- How can you turn intelligent objects into additional channels to your existing B2C and B2B customers?

- How can you win new customers and generate new revenue streams through automated data exchange between intelligent objects and machines?
- How could you increase the benefit for your existing customers with current and new channels?

7.10   Channels and Services and Data in the Cloud (Field C3)

Companies can advertise and offer their products and services around the clock, regardless of the location of their B2C and B2B customers. Tailor—made offerings are made possible by collecting and correlating historical customer data with external data, as well as a more efficient use of resources and higher productivity. Online platforms such as eBay and the Scout24 portfolio make markets more transparent and often more efficient for suppliers and consumers.

What Does this Mean for you?

- How could you digitalize channels to communicate with your customers more intensively and independently of time and place?
- How can digital platforms be used as additional channels to reach your most important customer segments?
- Which digital technologies enable you to deliver products and services to your customers as efficiently as possible?

7.11   Customer Relations and Networked People (Field A4)

Interaction with individual customers and communities using digital technologies enables suppliers to establish a better understanding of their needs and expectations. Social networking helps to turn prospects into customers, limit churn and increase satisfaction with products and services. Airbnb provides a community marketplace where people can advertise, discover and book accommodation online, and the community of the software manufacturer Workday provides implementation partners with exclusive information from experts and enables customers to share experiences.

What Does this Mean for you?

- How can you use social networks to better understand the wishes, needs and expectations of your existing customers?
- Do professional online communities help to find new customers and reduce customer churn?
- Can the value of your offering be increased for your existing customers through social networks?

7.12   Customer Relations and Intelligent Objects (Field B4)

With the use of intelligent objects, customers establish initial relationships with suppliers whose applications—if they are tailor—made for a device, for example—are often a good starting point for a customer relationship. This makes it more difficult for competitors to place their offerings. The data obtained enable suppliers to get to know the behavior of their prospects and customers better and to submit more suitable offers. Apple's seamless integration of hardware, operating system, and applications helps to motivate users to purchase additional hardware and software.

What Does this Mean for you?

- How can you win new customers with the help of intelligent objects?
- How can the devices already used by your customers support the sale of additional services?
- Which components of intelligent objects help to increase the benefits currently perceived by your customers?

7.13   Customer Relations and Services and Data in the Cloud (Field C4)

Digital services in the cloud help suppliers to retain their customers and keep the interest for new offerings on a high level. They can thus address customers at the right time, in the right place and with the messages that are relevant to them. Partner companies of Star Alliance and Payback—according to TNS Emnid the number—three—card in the wallets of German customers—use the exchange of customer data to increase customer loyalty, communicate their brands and generate higher revenues (Payback 2017).

What Does this Mean for You?

- How can you increase the satisfaction of your existing customers by using digital services?
- How can the acceptance of your customers for the collection and processing of data possibly be increased?
- To which extent can digital technologies support your existing customers in using your products and attract new interesting customers?

7.14   Revenue Streams and Networked People (Field A5)

Revenues are generated by controlling access to communities, networks and digital platforms and by using data from individual customers and companies. The ride—hailing company Uber generates revenue in over 500 cities by controlling access to suppliers through its partner app and is, like Airbnb and LinkedIn, a good example of a platform business model that benefits both suppliers and consumers (Uber 2017).

What Does this Mean for You?

- How can you generate recurring revenue streams with newly created digital connections of people and organizations?
- What would be the concrete added value of digital connections of companies for you?
- Which price models are attractive enough for your customers and partners and interesting enough for you?

7.15   Revenue Streams and Intelligent Objects (Field B5)

Intelligent objects and their benefits for previously identified customer segments allow providers to establish additional revenue streams. Product offerings which have been expanded to include digital services, such as HILTI Fleet Management, offer customers not only flexibility and transparency but also simplified budgeting and financial planning. With products such as Hue White Ambiance, Philips generates premium prices and makes it easy for customers to install and operate them (Hilti 2017 and Philips 2017).

What Does this Mean for you?

- Which of your previous revenue models can be replaced by the monetization of intelligent objects?
- Can intelligent objects possibly generate new revenue streams through interaction with your prospects and customers?
- How can a transparent and comprehensible revenue model be designed for your customers?

7.16   Revenue Streams and Services and Data in the Cloud (Field C5)

Digital services generate revenues around the clock and independent of the location of B2C and B2B customers. Subscription models such as the Handelsblatt offer described above or pay—per—use models—in which customers are only charged for the usage—offer the advantage that neither acquisition costs nor capital lockup are incurred. Apple's iTunes and AppStore applications generate recurring revenues from downloads, while Amazon offers its B2C and B2B customers unused and scalable computing capacity for usage—based payment through its Amazon Web Services online service.

What Does this Mean for you?

- What specific advantages do pay—per—use models offer for your current customer segments?
- Which basic conditions and parameters for the changeover to these models would be acceptable for your customers—and for you?
- How can digital services contribute to scaling your existing business model?

Summary

Digitalization is on one hand causing one of the greatest transformations in industry since the third industrial revolution in the 1970s, on the other hand a huge paradigm shift that is already creating and will continue to create turbulences and opportunities. In order to be able to take a chance of this transformation, to take advantage of the changed rules of the game, to adapt processes sensibly and to make current and future business models workable, a meaningful mix of proven and new tools is necessary.

The Business Model Canvas supports organizations in preparing for future challenges by providing a comprehensible starting point for the development, discussion, validation and selection of possible future business models. The digital elements presented - networked people, intelligent objects, services and data in the cloud - take the specifics of business processes and models in the context of Industry 4.0 into account and make the relationships transparent. The Digital Matrix combines the building blocks of a business model with the key elements of digitalization in order to create a working framework and offers a glimpse beyond the horizon by providing both relevant questions and a framework for the "translation" of ideas into business processes and models that will benefit equally customers and suppliers.

© Springer Fachmedien Wiesbaden GmbH, part of Springer Nature 2021   41
R. Ematinger, *From Industry 4.0 to Business Model 4.0*, Springer essentials,
https://doi.org/10.1007/978-3-658-32400-1_8

What You Learned From This *essential*

- Real-life and current examples that give you useful impulses for using the changed rules of the game and discovering patterns for new business and revenue models.
- Five promising patterns of business processes and business models, including examples of applications, which will give you food for thought about your current and future offers.
- Tried and tested tools such as the Business Model Canvas and the Digital Matrix, with which you can outline and discuss business models and use the developments of Industry 4.0 for your good ideas.
- Last but not least, your answers to the questions in the "What does this mean to you?" boxes that will help you to successfully transfer them into the reality of your organization.

© Springer Fachmedien Wiesbaden GmbH, part of Springer Nature 2021   43
R. Ematinger, *From Industry 4.0 to Business Model 4.0*, Springer essentials,
https://doi.org/10.1007/978-3-658-32400-1

References

Bargs-Stahl, Evelyn. 2016. Selbstlernende Systeme–Lebensmittelindustrie 4.0.idw-online. de/de/news651070. Accessed 06 Aug 2017.

Bitkom. 2015. Big Data und Geschäftsmodell-Innovationen in der Praxis – 40+ Beispiele. www.bitkom.org/Publikationen/2015/Leitfaden/Big-Data-und-Geschaeftsmodell-Innovationen/151229-Big-Data-und-GM-Innovationen.pdf. Accessed 06 Aug 2017.

Business Insider. Consumer and Office Robot Market. 2014. intelligence.businessinsider. com/consumer-and-office-robot-market-2014-5. Accessed 06 Aug 2017.

Cao, Jing, und Cortez, Michelle. 2016. IBM Extends Health Care Bet With Under Armour, Medtronic. www.bloomberg.com/news/articles/2016-01-07/ibm-extends-reach-into-health-care-with-under-armour-medtronic. Accessed 06 Aug 2017.

Chesbrough, Henry. 2010. Business Model Innovation–Opportunities and Barriers. *Long Range Planning* 43 (2): 354–363.

Christ, Ginger. 2014. 2013 IW Best Plants Winner: Harley-Davidson–Driving a Future of Excellence. www.industryweek.com/iw-best-plants/2013-iw-best-plants-winner-harley-davidson-driving-future-excellence. Accessed 06 Aug 2017.

European Design. 2017. Illustration nach einer Bildschirmkopie der App. https://europeandesign.org/submissions/swarovski-crystal-collection-app-for-b2b/. Accessed 06 Aug 2017.

Finch, Jeremy. 2015. What is Generation Z.www.fastcoexist.com/3045317/what-is-generation-z-and-what-does-it-want. Accessed 06 Aug 2017.

Goodwin, Tom. 2015. The Battle Is For The Customer Interface. www.techcrunch. com/2015/03/03/in-the-age-of-disintermediation-the-battle-is-all-for-the-customer-interface. Accessed 06 Aug 2017.

Hilti. 2017. Konzentrieren Sie sich auf Ihr Kerngeschäft – wir kümmern uns um Ihre Geräteflotte. www.hilti.de/content/hilti/E3/DE/de/services/tool-services/fleet-management. html. Accessed 06 Aug 2017.

IBM. 2010. IBM Global CEO Study 2010.www-935.ibm.com/services/de/ceo/ceostudy2010. Accessed on 06. Aug. 2017.

© Springer Fachmedien Wiesbaden GmbH, part of Springer Nature 2021
R. Ematinger, *From Industry 4.0 to Business Model 4.0*, Springer essentials,
https://doi.org/10.1007/978-3-658-32400-1

————. 2015. Effizienz schlägt Vielfalt-Industrie 4.0 gelingt schrittweise. www-01.ibm. com/common/ssi/cgi-bin/ssialias?subtype=WH&infotype=SA&htmlfid=IDW12349DE DE&attachment=IDW12349DEDE.PDF. Accessed 06 Aug 2017.

Innocentive. 2017. In the News. www.innocentive.com/in-the-news. Accessed 06 Aug 2017.

Intel. Guide to IoT Infographic. 2015. www.intel.com/content/dam/www/public/us/en/images/iot/guide-to-iot-infographic.png. Accessed 06 Aug 2017.

John Deere. 2017. John Deere Financial–Wir machen Produktivität erschwinglich. www. deere.de/de_DE/buying_and_financing/product_financing/agriculture_financing/agriculture_financing.page. Accessed 06 Aug 2017.

Just Park. 2017. The Most Popular Ideas in the Sharing Economy. www.justpark.com/creative/sharing-economy-index.Z. Accessed 06 Aug 2017.

Lufthansa. 2016. Lufthansa baut digitale Gepäckservice-Angebote aus. http://newsroom. lufthansagroup.com/de/meldungen/2016/q1/lufthansa-baut-digitale-gepaeckservice-angebote-aus.html. Accessed 06 Aug 2017.

Martin, Richard. 2016. Tesla-Solar City Success Depends on Battery Technology That Doesn't Yet Exist. www.technologyreview.com/s/601757/tesla-solarcity-success-depends-on-battery-technology-that-doesnt-yet-exist. Accessed 06 Aug 2017.

Memmel, Martin. 2015. Mehrwert und Mehrwertgenerierung. In *Smart Data Geschäftsmodelle*, Hrsg. FZI Forschungszentrum Informatik, 7–9. Berlin.

Mulholland, Andy. 2015. Internet of Things; what happens when 'sense' needs the 'respond' to come from an existing 'legacy' enterprise application? www.constellationr.com/content/internet-things-what-happens-when-sense-needs-respond-come-existing-legacy-enterprise. Accessed 06 Aug 2017.

Osterwalder, Alexander, and Yves Pigneur. 2010. *Business Model Generation – A Handbook for Visionaries, Game Changers, and Challengers*. Hoboken: Wiley.

Payback. 2017. Über Payback–Daten und Fakten. www.payback.net/de/ueber-payback/daten-fakten. Accessed 06 Aug 2017.

Philips. 2017. Das smarte Lichtsystem für dein Zuhause. www.philips.de/c-m-li/hue-persoenliche-kabellose-beleuchtung/hue-white-ambiance. Accessed 06 Aug 2017.

PwC. 2015. PwC-Studie: Share Economy. www.pwc.de/de/digitale-transformation/pwc-studie-share-economy.html. Accessed 06 Aug 2017.

Ramge, Thomas. 2015. *Die drei Zauberworte–Disruption*. Netzwerkeffekt: Plattform. www.brandeins.de/archiv/2015/handel/disruption-plattform-netzwerkeffekt-die-drei-zauberworte-neue-wirtschaft. Accessed 06 Aug 2017.

Ripton, JT. 2015. The Small Business Guide to Alternative Financing, www.digitalistmag. com/smb/2015/02/09/the-small-business-guide-to-alternative-financing-02180329. Accessed 06 Aug 2017.

Rolls-Royce. 2012. Rolls-Royce celebrates 50th anniversary of Power-by-the-Hour. www. rolls-royce.com/media/press-releases/yr-2012/121030-the-hour.aspx. Accessed 06 Aug 2017.

Schwab, Klaus. 2016. The Fourth Industrial Revolution: what it means, how to respond. www.weforum.org/agenda/2016/01/the-fourth-industrial-revolution-what-it-means-and-how-to-respond. Accessed 06 Aug 2017.

Smiley, Minda. 2016. 'It's only going to get bigger' – How Under Armour is planning to revolutionize the connected fitness space with the rise of wearables. www.thedrum.com/

news/2016/03/10/its-only-going-get-bigger-how-under-armour-planning-revolutionize-connected-fitness. Accessed 06 Aug 2017.

Solis, Brain. 2015. Disruptive Technology Trends 2015–2016.de.slideshare.net/briansolis/brand-innovators-2015-trends. Accessed 06 Aug 2017.

Swarovski. 2017. Swarovski's Crystal Collection App. http://professional.swarovski.com/Portal.Node/content/crystals/collection/crystal_collection_app/Collection.en.html. Accessed 06 Aug 2017.

TBO. 2017. (Handesblatt 10): Handesblatt 10 Award Winning App. tbointeractive.com/project/handelsblatt-10-app-fuer-iphone-und-android-smartphones. Accessed 06 Aug 2017.

Tesla Team. 2016. Tesla Makes Offer to Acquire Solar City. www.tesla.com/blog/tesla-makes-offer-to-acquire-solarcity. Accessed 06 Aug 2017.

Uber. 2017. Sei dein eigener Boss. www.uber.com/de/drive. Accessed 06 Aug 2017.

von Schoenebeck, Gudrun. 2015. Stahlbrücke in Amsterdam von Robotern ausgedruckt. www.ingenieur.de/Themen/3D-Druck/Stahlbruecke-in-Amsterdam-Robotern-Ort-ausgedruckt. Accessed 06 Aug 2017.

Westermann, George, et al. 2016. The Digital Advantage–How digital leaders outperform their peers in every industry. www.capgemini.com/resource-file-access/resource/pdf/The_Digital_Advantage__How_Digital_Leaders_Outperform_their_Peers_in_Every_Industry.pdf. Accessed 06 Aug 2017.

Zipkin, Nina. 2015. Here's What the Future of Work Looks Like to Millennials and Generation Z. www.entrepreneur.com/article/247115. Accessed 06 Aug 2017.